Baby's Here!
Who Does What?

How to split the work without splitting up

Duncan Fisher OBE

BABY'S HERE! WHO DOES WHAT?

How to split the work without splitting up

Copyright © Duncan Fisher, June 2010

All Rights Reserved

ISBN 978-1-905550-05-0

First published June 2010 by:
GS Press
The Old Vicarage
Myddfai, Llandovery
Carmarthenshire
SA20 0JE

Printed in Great Britain by:
HSW Print
Tonypandy
Rhondda
CF40 2XX

Baby's Here!
Who Does What?

How to split the work without splitting up

Duncan Fisher OBE

For Clare, Miriam and Abigail

ACKNOWLEDGEMENTS

Thanks to Clare for reading the text and putting up with me at home when I gave up on leading a balanced life in order to write about one. And to Miriam and Abigail for looking after the new puppy, Lottie, who would otherwise have eaten my computer. And, of course, were it not for Abigail and Miriam, I would not have written a book like this.

Thanks to Zelda West-Meads at the *Mail on Sunday* and her daughter, Caroline West-Meads, for reading the text and knocking more shape into it.

Thanks to David Taylor for designing the book to a completely unreasonable deadline and Carroll Nunnerley and Ric Foot at GS Press for helping to get the thing published. Also to Martha Halford-Fumagalli and Tom Beardshaw for helping with the marketing. And to 'JAKe' for the illustrations (www.jake-art.com).

Two books inspired me more than any other to write this book and I would like to thank both authors for writing them: Phil and Carolyn Cowan, authors of *When Partners Become Parents* and Sarah Hrdy, author of *Mothers and Others.*

Contents

Baby's here!
Who does what?

talking

sharing boxing & coxing

work pressure

sleep-walk changes

muddling through

pride cavemen

magic relationships

Why I wrote this book

When Clare and I had our first daughter in 1996, I became so fascinated by the whole modern parenting thing that I made it my job and have been studying it ever since. I discovered that the experience of our family is typical, we had very little idea of the right way to do things and we have muddled through as things changed from week to week, month to month, year to year. Sometimes we have got it right, sometimes not. The best thing I ever did – looking after our babies by myself on certain days of the week – came about by chance as our jobs moved around. I had no idea what a privilege this was until I fell into it by mistake.

I think that this 'muddling through'
is what being a family is all about
– there is no right way to do it and every
family is different. Working things out,
messing it up, starting again, constantly
boxing and coxing because there is
always far too much to do, being too
tired, feeling guilty, living on the edge
– this is what being a 21st century
parent is all about – as well as the total
magic of having children growing up
around us. I then learned that this isn't
just 21st century family life. This is also
what we did when mankind lived in
caves – which made me feel a bit better
about it!

> I think that this 'muddling through' is what being a family is all about – there is no right way to do it and every family is different

We can drift, like sleep-walkers, into patterns that make us unhappy

Experts have done a lot of thinking and research about how families organise their lives. It's interesting and useful, but we ordinary parents rarely get to know about it, because the 'parenting' books, the newspapers, the TV programmes all talk about babies as if they're only mum's business. We hardly ever hear about the thousands of things that mothers and fathers work out together every day to make family life go round.

I have written this book because I want to share the things I have discovered during 13 years of working on this issue – things that would have helped my own family if we had known about them earlier.

Time to talk?

Only one in five couples say their relationship gets better after a baby is born and a whopping two in three say their relationship gets worse

Babies are exhausting like nothing else; and in around one in six families, at least one of the parents gets depressed within a few months of the birth, which is particularly upsetting when you are both supposed to be so happy about the baby. With the tiredness and stress, we can drift, like sleep-walkers, into patterns that make us unhappy with ourselves and with each other. We stick with what we think we *should* do; we can't see out of the box at what we *could* do. And the longer we sleep-walk, the harder it is to change things. Only one in five couples say their relationship gets better after a baby is born and a whopping two in three say their relationship gets worse. One in three children experience their parents' separation before they reach the age of 16; and couples with children are much more likely to split than couples without children. What's more, almost one child in three who lives with both their birth parents sees their father as quite a distant figure and doesn't feel close to him.

THE CHALLENGES OF A NEW BABY

- No sleep
- No time together
- Changing relationship
- Work pressure
- Financial pressure
- Different ideas about bringing up children
- Depression
- Different styles of communication

We are pressured by society into thinking that what comes first is our children, and that our relationship with each other can wait. In a recent opinion poll however, 70 per cent of teenagers said that their parents' 'getting on well together' was critical to their own happiness but only 30 per cent of parents thought this was important. The teenagers are right. A survey of 7000 children in 2009 by the Children's Society found that the biggest influence on children's happiness is family relationships.

So, this book has one main message: don't sleep-walk – talk. There are no catch-all solutions. Human beings are incredibly good at being creative and adaptable when it comes to looking after children – we have evolved that way – so the only way and the best way is to work it out for ourselves. And that means talking, the one thing that really gets squeezed when there are babies about.

I hope this book can make clear some of the hidden pressures we families face, and how these can be dealt with, so that we find it easier to get to the root of the big question: what do we – both of us – want for our own family?

Who does what?

Most of us reduce the priority we give to our own relationship when a baby arrives. This is a mistake

How this book is organised

Chapter 1: Sharing – a real possibility?

This is not a hard sell – not everyone has to share earning and caring more or less equally. But most of us *need* to share to some extent – yet how, why and whether this is done is rarely talked about outside of our families (and often not enough within them). This chapter raises some thoughts for discussion at the kitchen table.

Chapters 2, 3 and 4: What stops sharing?

How work divides mothers and fathers. How beliefs and attitudes make it difficult to give up the roles we think men and women should play. How worries about men looking after children and women letting their children down if they work can

get in the way of sharing when sharing could actually make everyone's lives easier and better.

Chapter 5: Keeping our relationship going

Why parents being happy with each other is so important to our children. Most of us reduce the priority we give to our own relationship when a baby arrives. This is a mistake.

Chapter 6: Is sharing natural?

In the debate about what mothers and fathers can and cannot do, there's often chat about what is and isn't 'natural' – how humans organised their lives when they hunted and gathered and lived in caves. So how did cavemen and cavewomen really organise their family lives? What is actually 'natural'? It turns out that mothers have not looked after their own children by themselves - caring for babies and children has been shared around in families since we came out of trees.

Most of us want to share more than we do

Mothers- and fathers-to-be usually think that once their baby is born they'll share the care. They know the father will soon be back at work, but they still imagine he'll be doing loads of childcare. This rarely happens – and both parents feel pretty miserable about it. One – typically dad, but not always – finds himself squeezed out of home into earning money. He can feel a second class parent. The other parent – typically mum, but not always – finds herself squeezed out of all but maybe a little paid work into caring for the baby. She can feel isolated and lonely as a result. And if they swap? Then you often get a mother feeling guilty at not caring enough and a father feeling inadequate at not earning enough!

Parents know the father will soon be back at work, but they still imagine he'll be doing loads of childcare. This rarely happens

> 'I have to say that it can be extremely stressful. Because my salary is more than my partner's I work full-time for good pay and full benefits. My partner works part-time without benefits. Immediately before and after work and on weekends I switch to being the daddy. There is virtually no in between. No personal time. No time for exercise, social activities, hobbies, interests. I work and I raise kids. I have two full-time plus jobs. I wish I could do one or the other, but it's not economically feasible. '
>
> **A full-time working father**

> 'I love the idea of switching back and forth depending on our needs and jobs. We've done that in our house and it seems to put everyone in a more understanding position of each other's role. '
>
> **A Mother**

PARENTS USUALLY TRY TO SHARE

- Half of mothers with children under one work, mostly part-time.
- Today's fathers do eight times more caring for babies and young children than their fathers did.
- In the first year, new fathers work shorter hours than other men.
- One third of fathers work flexibly to spend more time with their children.
- Mums and dads both worry about getting the balance right between work and home.
- Two out of three mothers think fathers don't do enough in the home. Two out of three fathers agree!

Kitchen table talk

Every chapter ends with kitchen table talk – questions to ask each other.

For this chapter there is only one question:

→ **Do you think we talk enough?**

Chapter 1

Sharing – a real possibility?

caring flexibility

new skills patience

empathy bonding

multi-tasking

couple time financial risk

earning

housework stress

modern lives

The benefits of being flexible

Sharing roles in families (that is, each parent taking a big part in caring for the house and children and bringing home the bacon) isn't for everyone. Some people shudder at the very idea. But of course all parents share to some extent – with each other, with family and with non-family people and organisations. And things change constantly as the children get older – particularly when school starts – and as mothers and fathers change their paid work.

Flexibility is an asset. This can be more difficult if we've adopted narrow roles early on. A father who has 'helped out' at home but never been in charge may not do it very well – or in ways that the children don't like. A mother who is not used to earning money, and suddenly has to, can find it tough getting a decent job, and may earn very little.

> **A father who has 'helped out' at home but never been in charge may not do it very well – or in ways that the children don't like**

Research has shown that it is the parents who have shared more early on who tend to be able to share better later.

Most of us feel that the balance in our lives is not right one way or the other – too much earning, too much caring, not enough time for each other or ourselves. And we can disapprove strongly about the balance in our partner's life.

Do babies mess up relationships?

- Two thirds of relationships get a lot worse after a new baby
- Couples *without* children are less likely to split up
- When baby arrives both parents tend to put their couple-relationship on to the back burner – mothers more quickly
- Fathers often make a bid for 'couple time', including sex, but this can be seen as putting unfair demands on the exhausted mother, rather than taking care of the relationship
- In the first two years after a baby is born 'who does what' in housework and childcare is the single issue most likely to cause rows and discontent
- Most couples are startled by how traditional their lives are becoming

AN EXPERIMENT – PRIORITIES

Two researchers in the USA, Philip and Carolyn Cowan, asked parents to draw charts showing how important different parts of their lives were to them – worker, friend, mother, father.

- They looked at the new parents' changed priorities
- They looked at each couple and measured how different they felt from each other
- They looked at how happy these women and men were

They found three things:

- A mother who makes motherhood so big a part of her life that everything else goes down the tubes tends to have lower self-esteem.
- The bigger the difference between the partners' 'priority charts', the unhappier they were with their relationship.
- The bigger the difference between the way the parents-to-be had hoped to live their lives and the way their lives were panning out afterwards, the unhappier they tended to be with their relationship.

[Ref: When Partners Become Parents, by Carolyn and Philip Cowan, published by Lawrence Erlbaum Associates in 2000]

There is no escape from these pressures. For as long as we have been in existence, caring and providing for children (who stay dependent on their parents far longer than the young of any other species) has required massive juggling and huge effort. And there is no one right way of doing things. Throughout history in all parts of the world, different societies (and, within those, different families) have done things in very varied ways.

The bigger the difference between the way parents-to-be hope to live their lives and the way their lives are panning out, the unhappier they tend to be with their relationship

But there is one truth that we rarely hear – that some form of sharing of roles does tend to make most parents happier. When fathers do a lot at home and mothers earn their own money, we tend to feel happier in ourselves, the relationship between us tends to be better, we tend to be less stressed – and our children tend to do better. What this tells us is that it is very important not to sleep-walk into traditional roles, but to think very carefully, and keep thinking carefully, about how and whether we can share things.

So, even if sharing is not for everyone, thinking about it is! To that end, here are some of the arguments in favour of some sharing that might affect how we weigh up the options.

Sharing earning and caring – the benefits for parents

If we share earning, the pressure on the wage-earner is less. If only one of us earns, or earns most of the money, the pressure is really on them: one slip and they let everyone down. They may be really bad-tempered and intolerant because of the pressure on them. And what happens if they lose their job?

Unless our jobs make us miserable, paid work can be really fulfilling for both of us. Paid work can bring structure to our lives, another place to shine and be valued and feel competent, a sense that we matter, wider horizons and opportunities to learn new skills and develop as people, another social life.

> ❛My wife earns loads. I have long wanted to write and make films. Once the children started school, I was able to invest in this and be the main carer of our children during the week.❜
>
> **A father**

'My partner has a totally dependable job in the health service and a good one. My work is all over the place – I am a serial entrepreneur. Income goes up and down. I just could not do what I do without her job.'
A father

'I have always wanted to be my own boss. When we had children and I had to take some time off, I could tell my manager at work was not happy. I took the plunge and left that job. We both invested our money in an interior design business that I ran from our house.'
A mother

'If I am out of a job, I can wait for a good one if my partner earns a decent wage.'
A father

'I was made redundant last year. My wife hasn't worked since our first child was born 20 years ago. Now what?'
A father

When we share the earning from early on, we are taking less financial risk. We are providing ourselves and each other with protection against a credit crunch or some other economic downturn; against separation or divorce; against our partner's death, serious illness, unemployment, old age.

When we share the caring from early on, our bond with our children is deeper. We know them better and they feel safer with us. We have had more influence on them and find they are growing up more like us. After separation, children who don't have a really close relationship with one of their parents are likely to side with the other. A father who works the whole time, in particular, is running a risk that one day he'll lose everything. If we haven't been hands-on with little ones, we are rarely in a good place when it comes to dealing with stroppy teenagers.

When, right from the beginning, we share the care of children, we learn new skills in patience, tact, multi-tasking and crisis management.

> **A father who works the whole time, in particular, is running a risk that one day he'll lose everything**

These are skills we need at work and in our friendships and family relationships. In Sweden, some companies encourage dads to take leave to look after children because they come back to work more effective employees.

Children keep the world in perspective and help us focus on what really matters. Being involved in children's activities – the classroom, pets, school trips, sports (and not just at weekends) can be serious fun. And we get just one chance: when childhood is over, it's over.

Women feel more valued when they work outside the home. When workplaces have a lot of women in them who feel they matter as much as men, women start to achieve more and help to make workplaces more flexible and happier. This has an impact down the generations. Parents sharing roles isn't just for now: it's for the future too. Childhood does not last very long compared to how long we work.

> **We get just one chance. When childhood is over, it's over. Childhood does not last very long compared to how long we work**

> ' My last boss was a jerk. Now I've been transferred to a bad division. But I can't afford to protest or change jobs. If I were married to someone with a real career, I wouldn't have to suck up twenty-four seven. I feel trapped, like my only option is to stay here. '
>
> **A father**
> Quoted in Getting To 50/50 (by Sharon Meers & Joanna Strober)

It's good for children – and adults – to see both parents in a caring role. Children often see caring as something that only women do, but if lots of fathers take their babies to clinics and toddlers to playgroups, use flexible working to collect their kids from school (and hang around to talk to the teachers and to other parents), then we set better role models for them. And if fathers don't do that and pretend to their employers that they have no demands on their lives that will interfere with work, then those same employers will expect them to be like that: to behave like distant, Victorian fathers. And when our boys and girls grow up, they too will be trapped in a society that expects parents to split their lives: one mainly earning; one mainly caring.

> If fathers pretend to their employers that they have no demands on their lives then those employers will expect them to be like distant, Victorian fathers

Sharing earning and caring – the benefits for the relationship

> ❝He is a great dad to his children. But when he comes home he says he needs the time to recover and relax and have time to himself, because work has been tough. But being at home has been tough too and I need a break. He always seems to win.❞
>
> **A mother**

If one of us does ALL the earning and one does ALL the caring and domestic work, it can feel unfair and we can feel unsupported by our partner. The one who earns the money tends to get the bigger say, and that can feel really unfair for the one who works just as hard all day at home, but for no money.

Both parents are more able to ask for what they need. When mothers earn as much or more than fathers, they feel able to ask them to do more of the housework and childcare. When fathers earn the same or less than mothers, they feel freer to focus more on their relationships with their children; and to have opinions about the best ways to raise them.

We become nicer when it's not all about work. Parents more engaged in home-making tend to be more sensitive and more loving. Parents who have learned to read their babies' cues tend to use those same skills with their partner – and to have a happier relationship with them.

We understand each other better. If we share roles, we understand far better what life is like for our partners and are able to be more supportive. For instance, if we both worked, in those (now fondly remembered) days BC (before children), we probably both had lots to talk about and many experiences in common. But if one of us is now exclusively working and the other exclusively caring, we may find that we gradually have less and less to talk about and little idea of what life is like for our partner.

> **Parents more engaged in home-making tend to be more sensitive and more loving**

> ‘I miss the days when my wife came home with stories about her work. Now every night, she tells me what's going on in pre-school. I know what she's doing is important and I like hearing about our son's day. But I miss the camaraderie we once had, when she was working too.’
>
> **A father**
> quoted in: Getting To 50/50 (by Sharon Meers & Joanna Strober)

We are more likely to stay together.

How modern relationships have changed! Until the 1990s, couples with more traditional roles had stronger marriages. But now the opposite is true. Parents who share roles are less likely to separate or divorce.

When fathers do a lot at home and mothers focus on paid work as well as raising children, couples are far more likely to stay together. In fact, today, couples who operate traditional roles are almost twice as likely to split up as those who divide things at least 60/40 (1).

Parents who share roles have more sex.

Yes, it's true! A US study of 360 men in 2006 found that when both parents work they tend to have more sex (2). Both were somehow more often in the mood and more connected.

(1) Lynn Prince Cook, Doing gender in context: household bargaining and the risk of divorce in Germany and the United Sates, *American Journal of Sociology* 112.2 (September 2006)

(2) *VoiceMale* by Neil Chethik, published by Simon & Schuster in 2006

> **Couples who operate traditional roles are almost twice as likely to split up as those who divide things at least 60/40**

Sharing earning and caring – the benefits for children

Children suffer when their parents are stressed. The less parents share their roles, the more stressed they tend to be. Parents' stress affects children badly. Stressed parents tend to be colder, more angry, less tolerant, less responsive to their partner and their children, less able to set limits for their children, and more likely to have poor relationships with them. Children with parents who fight or argue a lot tend to do worse in school and in their friendships. Stress at work can of course 'spill over' into stress at home too – with all these same bad outcomes – but it's less common when both parents earn and both support each other at home.

Creating a network for your children's futures. One of the benefits of working (apart from money!) is the contacts we make there that can help our children. As children grow up and become workers themselves, they often make use of the connections their parents have made through their work. When both parents work, children have two sets of contacts to draw on.

Children have stronger bonds with both parents. Numerous surveys of children show many of them saying they don't get to spend enough time with their fathers. They don't generally complain about not seeing enough of their mothers. However, they want their mothers to be less stressed. When parents share earning and caring, mums tend to be less stressed and dads spend more time with their children. Children get what they want and need.

> **Children say they don't get to spend enough time with their fathers and they want their mothers to be less stressed**

Kitchen table talk
Questions to ask each other:

 **Do you think I do enough or too much housework/childcare/earning?**

 Do you feel under too much pressure with housework/childcare/earning?

 [To the main earner] Do you wish you could be more part of our children's lives?

Chapter 2

Work – how it divides us

flexible working

maternity leave

time with children

children's sickness

childcare costs

extra money

commuting working late

paternity leave

What we want from our work/ home balance...

In most families, dad carries on a paid job after the baby is born and it is mum's job to juggle both the care of children and the home and earning any 'extra' money the family needs. If childcare costs get high, parents usually think about stopping this 'extra' earning so that mum can save on childcare costs – instead of doing it by dad reducing his full-time hours or working flexibly. In some families, mum is the main earner and dad the main carer.

A lot of us are unhappy with our work/home balance – we think we work too much or not enough and we think our partners work too much or not enough

A lot of us are unhappy with our work/home balance – we think we work too much or not enough and we think our partners work too much or not enough.

- More than half of us say the arrangements we make are not what we would choose.
- More than half of fathers of one-year-olds think they spend too much time at work and not enough time with their baby.
- About 6 in 10 of us think fathers should spend more time caring for young children.

Which family are you?

If each of you do this by yourself, do you fill it in the same?

	Too much	Just right	Not enough
Mum works			
Dad works			

and what actually happens...

Doing one thing all or most of the time and feeling totally responsible for it is stressful

When children come along both parents tend to run around from morning to night, travelling to work, working, travelling home, shopping, picking up children, catching up on housework and then trying to snatch some sleep. Both parents tend to cut down on 'personal time' – everything except paid work, housework and caring for their children (and sometimes other relatives too) gets forgotten. They also have less leisure time and sleep less!

Before children, most couples tend to share paid work and housework. It's after children are born that the roles split.

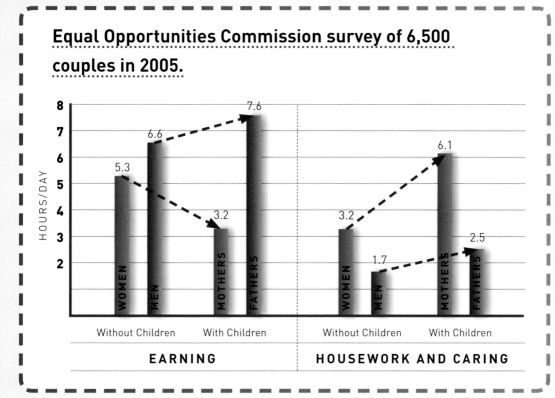

Equal Opportunities Commission survey of 6,500 couples in 2005.

HOURS/DAY

EARNING — Without Children: WOMEN 5.3, MEN 6.6; With Children: MOTHERS 3.2, FATHERS 7.6

HOUSEWORK AND CARING — Without Children: WOMEN 3.2, MEN 1.7; With Children: MOTHERS 6.1, FATHERS 2.5

Doing one thing all or most of the time and feeling totally responsible for it is stressful.

- Any parent who works 45 hours or more is likely to feel stressed – and they almost certainly won't be spending enough quality time with their partner and children to keep those relationships on track.
- Any parent who is home alone with the children for most of the working week is likely to feel stressed, unsupported and lonely.

A SURPRISING MYTH

Because often nowadays both parents work, people assume that parents are on average spending less time with their children than they used to. Wrong!

Both parents (including most working mothers!) are on average spending more time interacting with their children than our parents spent with us. This is because in many families:

- Children used to play outside more.

- Mothers spend much less time on cooking and housework than their mothers and grandmothers did, and are using that time to spend with their children.

- Fathers spend more time on cooking and housework than their fathers and grandfathers did and this frees mothers up to be more with the children.

- Men don't go out to the club/pub for their leisure nearly as much as they used to: they spend their leisure time at home – near (and often with) their partners and children.

- Both parents tend to cut down on everything except work and looking after the children.

Don't be late back. I need to get to my course
The school needs me to teach next week. Can you do nights that week?
Boss said I can work 4 long days instead of 5 normal. One more day of childcare sorted!
Managed all shopping with Eli awake! Did the phone calls while she was asleep
Tommy's sick. I'll collect him but need to do my emails after bath-time

How workplaces squeeze women out & men in and how to manage it

There is a big economic incentive to divide roles with one parent working a lot more than the other

Full-time jobs are almost always better paid and have better career prospects. Flexible or part-time work tends to pay less and can mean missing out on promotion. Most families feel they need at least one partner to be working full-time with all the advantages that brings. And because they feel that two full-time working parents can't provide enough family time, they go for one full-time job and one part-time job – even if they don't want to. There is a big economic incentive to divide roles with one parent working a lot more than the other.

Although new employment law is slowly changing attitudes, employers often expect women, not men, to change their working patterns for children.

This distinction often starts even before babies are born. Employers may be more likely to line young men up for promotion and invest more in training them than they do in training young women. They tend to celebrate the men's successes more than the women's. Young men and women see this – men see they have a brighter and better paid working future, women see they are more likely to be sidelined.

This can lead to some women having less confidence at work – not necessarily a big crisis, just a series of small thoughts and decisions that are a bit different from the thoughts and decisions that men make.

Employers tend to expect women, and not men, to deal with crises at home.

Good reading: *Getting to 50/50* (by Sharon Meers & Joanna Strober) explains more about the pressures on mothers and why sharing with fathers is part of the answer.

An experiment – employers tend to expect women, and not men, to deal with crises at home

Employers were given different job applications to assess. In the application the person wanted to work part-time and was a parent. But some of the applications were given a woman's name and some a man's name. The application was more likely to be successful if it was in the man's name. It is just assumed that, when it comes to childcare crises, children's sickness, school activities, it will be mum, and not dad, that is called out of work to sort them out.

It is just assumed that, when it comes to childcare crises, children's sickness, school activities, it will be mum, and not dad, that is called out of work to sort them out

Many employers resist parents who ask for flexible working – and are more likely to resist a request from a man than from a woman, even though sometimes flexible working could help their business.

Men are more afraid of asking for flexible working than women are (even when, in fact, the employer would be fine about it).

Sometimes work is organised so that the only people who can get to the top are those who do not have to do anything in life other than work. These people are seen as being successful.

They are not seen as losers who need to get a life!

If an unemployed woman goes into an employment office, they will ask her if she is a mother and then she will be offered special help to find a job that fits her role. An unemployed man looking for a job won't be asked if he has children.

After baby number two, the roles often become even more established. When one parent is already earning less after the birth of the first baby, and another baby comes along, it is even easier to decide who should keep working and who should stay at home.

YOUR RIGHT TO ASK FOR FLEXIBLE WORKING

Both mothers and fathers have a right to ask for flexible working. This doesn't sound like much but it's actually quite a big deal – once you've formally 'asked' an employer has to give a really good reason for turning you down, or risk an Industrial Tribunal.

How the law discriminates

In the UK, the law actually makes it impossible for fathers to care for their babies in the first year without giving up their job altogether. Only mums get the right to long-term leave with their jobs held open while they're on leave.

Dad has a right to:

- two weeks at £123/week

Mum has a right to:

- six weeks at 90 per cent pay, plus

- 33 weeks at £123/week, plus

- 13 weeks, right to time off without pay.

This is just about the biggest difference between the leave available to mums and dads in the world.

Compare it with Iceland.

Dad gets 13 weeks well-paid leave, and

Mum gets 13 weeks well-paid leave, and

Together they get 13 weeks to divvy up as they want

How caring is less valued than earning

In the UK, caring for children is seen as less important than paid work.

Fathers who want to care for their children tend to be seen as less important then fathers who do not. When a politician is sacked, we are told he wants to spend 'more time with his family'.

This is now happening to mothers – many mothers who want to spend more time with their children are feeling pressured to stay working.

CHANGES YOU CAN MAKE

- You have a legal right to ask for flexible working. Even carving out one afternoon a week, in exchange for more work at another time in the week, gives a chance for a special regular time with the children and saves on childcare.

- If you are not working, can you fit in some study time to get ready for more interesting work later? Your partner may need to guarantee regular working hours to let you do this.

- Can you divide things into "can do with baby awake" (e.g. shopping) and "can't do with baby awake" (e.g. phone calls, flopping out after work) and then organise the whole day on that basis?

- If work demands that one of you give up the chance of a deep relationship with your children, or if caring for the children is knocking out any chance for you to ever get your dream job, can one or both of you change your work?

- Can you move home to somewhere where housing or rent or childcare is cheaper?

- If one or both sets of grandparents are willing to help with childcare, can you move nearer to them?

Kitchen table talk

Questions to ask each other:

→ Do you think I am working too much, about right, not enough?

→ Are you happy with the amount of money I am earning or not earning?

→ If the cost of childcare is more than one of our salaries, should one of us earn less and do more caring of the child? If so, which one?

→ Should one of us stop working altogether or do we both keep our hands in at work for when our children are older?

→ Should we move house to a cheaper place or nearer relatives, or move to where we could earn more?

And questions to ask ourselves:

→ Am I happy enough with my job to make it worth continuing?

→ Can I work more flexibly or different hours, even a little bit?

→ If I want to work a lot, is my partner happy to take over everything at home and work much less? – and am I confident that my relationship with my children won't take a serious hit?

→ If I want to be a stay-at-home parent, is my partner happy to spend most of his or her time at work – and am I prepared to take the financial and other risks of being dependent on their income?

Chapter 3

Moving over to let the other parent in – the challenge

negotiation

practice efficiency

top parent feeling guilty

boxes in our heads

work addiction sharing

caring instinct

How do you want to share?

Should mum be in charge of caring?

34% of mothers say yes
23% of fathers say yes

Is mum in charge of caring?

86% of mothers say yes
69% of fathers say yes

(Figures taken from an Equality and Human Rights Commission survey of 2,600 parents in 2009)

Over half of us say that the way we organise family life is not how we would choose

Why do we believe in one thing and then do something different? On the day I was writing this chapter, the *Daily Mail* published an article, *Paternity leave? Any man who says he wants it is really a liar.* That's one possible explanation for the difference! But are we mothers and fathers actually lying when so many of us say that caring should be shared between parents?

I don't think so. I think that when we want one thing and do another, it is because we are under pressure. It is not just the external pressures like work, but pressures in our heads – things we think we 'should' do and feel bad about if we don't. Over half of us say that the way we organise family life is not how we would choose.

If you fill this table in separately, do you agree with each other? Does how you think it should be fit the reality?

	Yes	No
Mum should be the main carer		
Dad should be the main earner		

Boxes in our heads: fathers

Men are expected to carry on working without changing their lives when they become fathers.

Nobody ever asks 'should a father go back to work after his baby is born?' or 'Should a mother go back to work so dad can do more of the childcare?'

People raise their eyebrows when fathers of young children stay at home – the opposite reaction to mothers of young children who stay at home.

Working long hours or 'sacrificing' time with the family to win in the wider world (as so many sportsmen do) is seen as macho: something to be regretted but (at the same time) the mark of a 'real man'.

Government expects fathers, not mothers, to work – with two weeks of poorly paid leave for fathers, compared to 39 weeks paid leave for mothers. In short, if a father needs to look after his baby, he has to leave his job.

> **Nobody ever asks: 'should a father go back to work after his baby is born?'**

Because 'providing for my family' is seen so much as the father's role, it's a lot easier for fathers to fall into working long hours. They can feel inadequate if they don't work long-hours, even if they hate their job and it makes them really unhappy.

Once we start working long hours, work can become addictive. This can happen to mothers too, but it is easier for fathers to get into this situation since fathers get approval for working long hours, and mothers face disapproval. It is very easy to find ourselves working the whole time and being unable to switch off. We may even tell ourselves 'it's for my children.'

Because unpaid work at home isn't valued as highly as paid work, the way we value ourselves often gets tied up with how we perform at work. We can measure what we get done at work more easily than at home, so we often get greater satisfaction at work.

'If we are going to make a difference as fathers we need to do it NOW. That decision is practical. It has more to do with bedtimes, Saturday football games, stories and hamburgers than it has to do with carving those times out of busy lives – today'

Rob Parsons
in 'The 60 Minute Father'

Children often seem ungrateful and can be more difficult to deal with than the most annoying colleague. If they feel they don't see enough of us they can play us up even more – and this can push us back into work. And if we don't get much practice being 'in charge' at home, it's easy to think that the other parent is simply better at it – and to leave the children to them.

Mothers tend to ask fathers to change their ways, more than fathers ask mothers to change. This is because mothers tend to be in charge at home, where they want the changes to happen. This can make fathers annoyed and they may withdraw into work.

All this is really sad – because no person in their old age ever said 'I wish I had spent more time at the office.'

If we don't get much practice being 'in charge' at home, it's easy to think that the other parent is simply better at it – and to leave the children to them

> **We don't necessarily have to assume that the dad's role is to work whatever the circumstances**

Today's grandfathers often tell their sons: 'Don't do what I did. Don't miss out on your children growing up because you believe that work is really where it's at. It's not.'

So when we sit down to work out who does what, we don't necessarily have to assume that the dad's role is to work whatever the circumstances. Thinking outside the box may help us see family life differently and even if we decide to follow quite traditional roles, at least we are doing it with our eyes open and we are ready to handle the downsides.

Good reading: *The 60 Minute Father* (by Rob Parsons) has great stuff on workaholism and the curse of leaving things till tomorrow, which never comes. It helps that you can read it in 60 minutes.

Can we both work and both do some days childcare?
Thanks for stepping in just then. I nearly lost it with baby and needed to cool off.
You are so good at getting her to sleep! What's the secret?
I want to go out with the girls - some bonding time for you!
I just have to do this project. Can you look after baby a bit more for the next two weeks?
You are so good with baby, can't you work a bit less?

Boxes in our heads: mothers

Mothers are **expected** to be the primary carer – the top parent, the best parent – and to be in charge of the home.

Mothers and fathers tend to believe that mothers have special skills with babies and children that fathers lack. Actually it is not as biological as this. Mothers are very different from each other with babies, and so are fathers. Men also have very strong caring instincts and, as humans, we are uniquely able to adapt to new roles. By far the biggest reason why one particular mother may be more skilled than the father is that she has had so much more practice.

When mothers do more childcare and housework, they tend to become better at it and feel they must be in charge otherwise it will fall apart or not be done 'properly'. Fathers can then end up believing this too.

> **Mothers are often made to feel as if they're abandoning their children just because someone asks the simple question: 'So who is looking after them?'**

Being top parent can make a mother feel good, even if at the same time she is feeling angry, overworked, lonely and put-upon.

Mothers who work are often made to feel guilty. Relatives and friends (and even people at work) can seem to suggest that they're abandoning their children just by asking the simple question, 'so who is looking after them?'

There are constant reports in the press about the dangers to children if mothers work – they'll supposedly get fat or fight the other kids at nursery or their teeth will rot. None of this research takes into account families where fathers and other family members do a lot of the care. When that's included the results look different: the key is that the child's *family* provides good enough care, not just the mother.

Because mothers are supposed to be the 'top parent', some mothers get jealous and insecure when their children get very attached to others –

whether the childminder or their father, or where the father has a natural flair for communicating with small children.

> **Good reading:** *Partnership Parenting* (by Kyle Pruett and Marsha Kline Pruett) goes into detail about the art of two parents agreeing how to bring up children.

> **An experiment – parental confidence:**
>
> Fathers were given a task to do with a small child. In one group the mother was present in the room. The fathers tended to ask the mother if they were doing it right. When the mother was not present, the father did the task more efficiently and more competently.
>
> Symptoms of not sharing responsibility:
>
> **'Please feed the children. And make sure...'**
>
> **'Did you brush his teeth for the full two minutes?'**
>
> **'Sorry, he's got a doctor's appointment. I forgot to say.'**

WHOSE SIDE ARE YOU ON?

A father:

'I'm a bit rattled about how unloved she can make me feel. She doesn't mean to, but she makes me feel incompetent, like a mediocre parent. She just has a way of correcting what I say and do... I can feel myself withdrawing and it scares me.'

His partner's viewpoint — the mother:

'I am surprised how often I feel annoyed at him when he's parenting our little girl. It's like he doesn't get who she really is, so I try to be helpful and steer him in the right direction. Then he gets this glazed look and I think he's gone off in his head.'

[Quoted in Partnership Parenting by Kyle Pruett and Marsha Kline Pruett]

The debate:

'What happens when you both want to be the stay-at-home parent? Somebody has to work – and is it fair to the mum to say that she has to be the one to work when she doesn't want to? That she has to leave the child she has carried for nine months because dad can take care of the baby just as well? I know I am supposed to favour these changes in fatherhood, but where does it leave the mum who would prefer the traditional division of labour?'

A mother

'Great, so where does that leave fathers who would prefer to avoid the traditional division of labour and do more at home? Do we have any say or must we just do what we are told? Next thing we know, we will be accused of not pulling our weight at home – we just can't win! Sorry, but this has to be NEGOTIATED! **'**

A father

' Yes, but if he's NEVER AROUND and keeps coming home later than he said he would, someone has to be in charge at home and it's not going to be him is it? I know what's going on in the house, he doesn't. That's the reality. He needs to step up before I can step aside. **'**

A mother

' I'm tired of hearing women and men complain that the infant just won't take to dad and that mum just doesn't get a break. Hand dad the baby carrier and send them for a walk... go to a film with a friend... this is not child abuse or damaging to your children... without it he will not start establishing a connection and bond to dad. **'**

A mother

' You get into a cycle of perfect efficiency which you think will fall apart if anyone else lays a finger on the child, and there's your poor partner hanging around saying, "Errrr, could I help?'" And you're saying, "No! You won't get it right!" **'**

A mother

' I work from home and do a lot round the house. My partner took lots of maternity leave for our second child. After a while I realised I was doing nothing round the house any more, just on my own working all the time. Both of us were on autopilot – we were far too tired to think. It was only when she went back to work part-time that a balance returned and I got back to spending proper time with both children – and back to the ironing. **'**

A father

The need to talk

In the end, it's not what we do that counts but how much we agree with each other about what we do. Thinking outside the box helps, even if we choose to go back into the box afterwards. And, in fact, if we do regularly think outside the box and question what we're doing, it's pretty certain that we will do some things differently.

> It's not what we do that counts, but how much we agree with each other about what we do

In fact, researchers find that just talking about these things makes couples happier.

But the stereotypes go deep, and 'busting' them can be really tricky. I've spent 13 years working on this and I still get caught out by the stereotypes and assumptions in my head.

I have a simple method I use to challenge this: whenever someone makes a generalization about mothers, I re-word it in my head as if it were about fathers – and then listen to what it sounds like. Often it sounds stupid.

And whenever someone makes a generalization about fathers, I re-word it in my head as if it were about mothers. That too often sounds stupid. This gives me the clue I need to understand the boxes in my head.

An example: We often say 'Should mothers go back to work?' I try 'Should fathers go back to work?' Why do these sound so different?

Barging ahead without thinking and discussion down the path we simply assume is the right one for us means we don't think about the downsides for both of us. What if one of us is really unhappy? They may simply be getting on with it, or they may have tried telling us and we haven't listened.

Families can break up because of tensions like this!

Kitchen table talk
Questions to ask each other:

 Main carer to main earner:

- **Do I sometimes forget to tell you important things about our child?**

- **Do I boss you about too much when you are looking after our child?**

 Main earner to main carer:

- **Do I sometimes organise work without thinking about how this will affect family life?**

- **Am I around enough to notice what needs doing?**

Both:

- **Do my assumptions about my own work role feel okay for you?**

- **Do my assumptions about my own caring role feel OK for you?**

- **What changes would you like to see?**

Chapter 4

Men and babies

bonds stereotypes
rough and tumble
mums & tots group
parenting instinct breastfeeding
man with a pram
biology

Are dads good for children?

On average, fathers do eight times more caring of children than 30 years ago and a man with a pram is not an unusual sight any more. Fathers everywhere are saying they want to be closer to their children than their fathers were to them.

Does this work for babies and children? And when should this closeness start – right at the beginning or only a bit later? And if we are both looking after our children, what do we do about the fact that we do some things differently from each other?

Are dads good for children? Yes. We all know that strong, happy relationships between mothers and their children are absolutely vital. What about fathers? Yes – it's the same: although children can grow up OK without a particularly good relationship with their dad (or mum) provided other people have raised them well, a bad or missing father-child relationship (like a bad or missing mother-child relationship) is a serious drawback.

After 40 years of research, experts are now clear that when a child has a loving and close relationship with their father (whether he lives with them full-time or not), that child tends to do better in all kinds of ways:

- Better at school
- More popular
- Less likely to get into trouble with the police, take drugs or become a teenage parent
- More likely to have stable and happy relationships with boyfriends and girlfriends
- Better mental health when they are adults

It is never too late to start being an involved father, but the earlier it starts the stronger the bonds

It is never too late to start being an involved father, but the earlier it starts the stronger the bonds and the more likely it is that the closeness will last through all the changes to come: babyhood, toddler-hood, school, adolescence, young adulthood. That's why experts say the best thing is for fathers to start on that closeness straight away – from the scans onwards. Some midwives encourage fathers go skin-to-skin with baby immediately after the birth. This causes a rush of prolactin – the falling in love hormone!

Parenting differently

When two people spend a lot of time looking after a baby or child, they develop their own ways of doing things. This can cause conflict and disagreement.

This is quite difficult to handle when mothers are expected to know all about parenting and be perfect at it from day one and fathers are expected to be clumsy and incompetent. We tend to assume that if we do things differently, it is because mum is getting it right and dad is not. In fact, good instincts with children are not the preserve of mothers. And experts have found that, when the mother is seen as 'the expert', fathers with good instincts often hang back – even when they can see that the mother in not parenting well and may be quite distressed.

Such fathers seem not to trust their own judgement, or perhaps they fear undermining their partner. Everyone misses out if this happens.

When I am out and about in town and I see parents, particularly when they are sitting in coffee shops trying to control young children, I can see the couples where both parents are at ease with the child and the couples where mum is definitely in charge. Sometimes the baby is sitting on her lap with its back to the father. Sometimes he's doing his bit, but looking anxiously at his partner. Sometimes the mother just cannot stop giving instructions. When I see this, I am always struck by how sheepish some of these fathers look, so different from how most men would like to appear in public.

Mothers are expected to know all about parenting and be perfect at it from day one, and fathers are expected to be clumsy and incompetent

A game...

Give a small child a puzzle that is just a bit too difficult for him or her. The child starts to get a little frustrated. What do we do?

One of us might help the child with a little 'cheating' – pushing the right piece under her nose and then congratulating her. The other might hold back, waiting for her to succeed and not giving in until she succeeds – and then congratulating her with perhaps more conviction.

The first approach is typically mum's (but by no means always) and the second approach is typically dad's (again not always). Is one way better than the other? Is the mum actually more attuned to the child and the dad less sensitive? Not if, in both cases, the child succeeds in the end.

> **A child will learn more - precisely because she is having experience of two different parenting styles**

Both parents have the same goal; that the child should end up happy. But in one scenario, the child may feel more secure and in the other more challenged. To get through life, the child needs both of these experiences. The child is learning more – precisely because she is having experience of two different parenting styles.

If we share, we are likely to argue about such things more. But that doesn't have to be a problem: arguing can actually help us feel closer in the end because we're involved in the same project – and disagreement can lead to new ways of doing things.

HERE ARE SOME OTHER THINGS THAT PARENTS ARE LIKELY TO DO DIFFERENTLY:

- Holding the baby – which way is the baby facing?
- Responding to a crying baby – how long before we give in?
- Responding to a child who *might* be hurt or might just be putting it on to get attention (or, of course, to get the blame pinned on their brother or sister!)
- Playing with a child – how much risk do we let the child face?
- How much we expect our children to tell us about what they are feeling before we respond – do we act to meet the child's need even before the child has worked it out, or wait till the child asks?

Why do we parent differently from each other?

Parents are different people with their own personal histories. So when two parents get together, you get a unique mix. Each also brings a range of experiences, interests and behaviours specific to their sex.

Having said that, there are very few Mr Typical Man and Ms Typical Woman. Dad might like to do some 'man things' round the house, but not all, and mum might like to do some of them instead. Equally, mum might like to do some woman things, but she might not like to do others. I confess I don't do much cooking, but I do the ironing. I do most of the house repairs but I don't touch the car. I bet in nearly every family there are things that we do 'the other way round'.

What we do depends on the situation we are in and this can change from week to week.

Take the playful dad (or mum) who swings his child around and throws them into the air. Rough and tumble is great for children – they adore it. But if a father is looking after a child all day long, he doesn't do rough and tumble all day. Rough and tumble is often about a father having only a short time with the children and needing to make it extreme to make the most of it.

In fact, a father who just does rough and tumble is the mark of the second-fiddle father – the one who is stuck on the edge doing his best to get a look in and have an effect. Children see through this in the end – they don't confide in people who are just jokers. Surveys of children constantly find them saying that they don't share their feelings with their fathers as much as they would like.

Rough and tumble is often about a father having only a short time with the children and needing to make it extreme to make the most of it. Children see through this in the end – they don't confide in people who are just jokers

Mothers and fathers both have to learn to care for their children

Mothers and fathers both have to learn to care for their children. Mothers don't automatically know how to care for babies to start with, but they get bucket loads of practice very fast. Fathers who get practice – even if not as much as mothers – quickly become skillful too. And when dads or mums feel skilled they tend to do a lot, which makes sense because the more confident we are at something the more we tend to do it. And the more we do, the more skilled we become . . .

The way we each behave with a child affects the way our partner behaves with them. Take a mother who is very protective of a baby. She will restrict what the father can do. Take a dad who is not confident with his child: he's likely to hang back and encourage his baby's mother to do more.

A lot depends on the baby. Babies are very different from each other and respond differently to adults – and different adults respond differently, too. For example, one parent may pay lots of attention to a fussy baby; the other may withdraw. That can set up a pattern quite quickly.

Finally, in the middle of all this there are sex-differences: what men do; what women do. But here's a challenge: when you spot a difference in the way you and your partner behave as mother or father, what's causing that difference? Is it biology or the way you've been brought up as male or female – or is it due to difference in personality or a difference in your situations? And if you think it is biology, is it really something you can't change? A hallmark of humans is our ability to adapt when we need to.

Stereotypes – attacking our confidence...

Stereotypes can be vicious little beasts. They attack us when we are down

I remember one night in particular. Our younger daughter was screaming and had decided that I was no good – only her mum would do and mum was trying to get some sleep. This had never happened with our first baby – I could always calm her down and that made me feel fantastic. But now I was shattered. I wanted nothing more than to go to sleep. And then the demons came out. Is this because I am a man? Am I actually biologically useless? Will I always be like this? Would it actually matter if I fell under a bus? I don't know how many people said to me 'but your daughter will be wild about you in no time at all' – this was no comfort that night; it meant nothing.

Or take the experience of some mothers. Mothers are expected to be perfect happy parents from the first minute. But what if they aren't? What if they feel nothing when they look at their new baby – and for some time afterwards? What if breastfeeding is really painful and hard? Does this mean they are flawed and useless mothers?

Stereotypes can be vicious little beasts. They attack us when we are down. They tell us we are failures at the very moment we most need support.

The best way of dealing with these stereotypes is to recognise them. These stresses and disappointments do not mean we are failed mothers or useless fathers; they are normal. In fact, they are very common nowadays – for most of the last 200,000 years, we brought babies up with lots of family around us to help, 24 hours a day. Not any more for most of us.

What if mothers feel nothing when they look at their new baby?

...and things we hide behind

But we also use stereotypes to hide behind our choices. If we can say we do something because of biology, then we don't have to change and everyone around us just has to take the consequences.

> If we can say we do something because of biology, then we don't have to change and everyone around us just has to take the consequences

In the week that I was writing this chapter, a chap wrote a long article in a national newspaper explaining why he did not want to help out at home. He liked work and that is what he wanted to do. He loved his children, he even taught them to read. But look after them all day? No way!

He justified this by rolling out the five standard stereotypes:

- Caring for babies and children is natural for mothers and not for fathers
- It's the mother's role to worry and to feel guilty about things
- The dog-eat-dog world of work requires skills that only men have
- Men cannot multi-task, only women
- Men find time with young children boring and women do not

Having decided that everything is down to biology, he could conclude that any man who says he feels differently is a liar. And so, everyone has to fall in with his way of doing things (particularly the mother of his children!)

Couples who operate traditional roles are almost twice as likely to split up as those who divide things at least 60/40

Busting the stereotypes

1. Caring for babies and children is natural for mothers and not for fathers. Untrue!

I have written a whole chapter on this – Chapter 6. The reality is that human fathers are actually genetically *programmed* to be able to look after babies: their hormones change when they are around pregnant women and when they care for babies and children. Their hormones don't change as much as women's of course (women are carrying the baby – and usually breastfeeding), but hormones don't change without a reason. And when a baby cries, men get just as upset as women. Their pulse races as much as a woman's does, they sweat, they feel as anxious – and they want to soothe that baby. Interestingly, if you video them, they don't *look* as upset as women – but hook them up to a lie detector (which measures heart rate, sweat and

Fathers are genetically programmed to be able to look after babies

so on), and you see their reactions are just the same.

2. Men cannot multi-task, only women. Untrue!

Research shows that men multi-task just as well as women (think of a restaurant manager or a film director – they never stop multi-tasking). When a person doesn't multi-task it's usually because they're not very confident about one or more of the tasks they're taking on OR because they see themselves as a helper, rather than the manager. Helpers tend to stick to one thing at a time.

> **Research shows that men can multi-task just as well as women**

3. Men find time with young children boring and women do not. Untrue!

Anyone who spends a lot of time with young children can find it boring and tough. That's one reason why full-time stay-at-home mums are more likely to be depressed than working mothers. Any person who spends too much time doing anything will start to react against it after a while. That's why we invented weekends and holidays and why we help each other.

4. When men say they want to be close to their children, they are lying. Untrue!

I come across this all the time. I was on the radio once, talking about paternity leave. An 'expert' told us that when men in Sweden take paternity leave, they use it to go hunting, not to spend time with their children. When I checked this out I found it to be completely false. The 'expert' couldn't accept that men could actually want to spend time with their kids.

> **Usually if men don't take paternity leave, it's not because they don't want to, it's because they can't afford to**

This lack of trust is why the British Government only gives men two weeks of paternity leave while giving mothers 52 weeks maternity leave. When men don't take their paternity leave (which is incredibly low-paid – at just £123 per week), the first thing people think is that they don't take it because they don't want it – not because they can't afford to take it. In fact, almost all men take time off when their children are born: it's just that they use annual leave, not paternity leave, because the annual leave is properly paid.

I have spent many years advising government about families and have learned to live with the suspicion that I must be in this for some selfish, hidden reason – in it for my 'rights' rather than because, like most of the women who do my kind of work, I'm a parent and I want to work on parenting professionally, as well as being a parent to my own children.

THE HALLMARKS OF GREAT PARENTING:

- Being able to love
- Being patient
- Being flexible
- Being unselfish
- Being sensitive to the needs of each particular child
- Being sensitive to the needs of the other parent
- Understanding children's development (so you don't expect too much or too little from them)
- Making time

These are things that women and men can do equally well.

What about breastfeeding?

Only mums can breastfeed. What does that mean for the rest of baby care?

Babies don't only need to eat! They need to be changed, bathed, rocked, cuddled, talked to, gazed at. This all starts as soon as they're born. Babies do not mind who does these things, or whether it's a man or a woman who does them, or several men or several women. A father can do all these things even if he's only around for a couple of hours a day. Even very new babies are not feeding or asleep for a big chunk of every day (and night!)

And even breastfeeding is not just mum's business. One of the biggest influences on whether a mother gets on well with breastfeeding is what she thinks the father thinks about breastfeeding and what he does or does not do to support it. Fathers are very important to the whole breastfeeding thing, even though they don't have breasts.

> So yes, only mums breastfeed. But breastfeeding takes more than just the mother and not only mothers can look after babies

Men in a women's world

If you are a man looking after a small child, you might well want to use some local playgroups, nurseries and Children's Centres because, like a new mum, you will need adult company too. But this can be daunting for fathers because these places are usually packed with women!

Ten years ago I helped to set up an organisation, the Fatherhood Institute, which helps family services to include fathers. I don't work for the Institute any more, but I asked them to name the top things that fathers should do to get the best out of nurseries, schools and playgroups.

Here is the advice from the experts:

1. Get yourself registered. Too often, nurseries, schools, even midwives, only take the father's name if he shows up (and sometimes not even then). So make sure whoever looks

> **Playgroups can be daunting for fathers because these places are usually packed with women**

after your child or interacts with you as a family has a record of your name, address and phone numbers – including your mobile. (If their form only has a space for the mother on it, ask them to take your details too, and keep them on your child's file.)

2. If there's a home visit by one of these professionals or a baby-clinic visit, *be there*. Two people hearing what is said and asking questions is better for your children than just one. You also need to get to know the professionals yourself, in case your family needs them one day.

3. Find out what is on offer through the local clinic, Children's Centre and so on – maybe baby massage, parent-baby groups, parenting courses, sessions on feeding or sleeping or first aid. Get in there, alone or with your partner. Get the knowledge. And you'll be helping other men: when you show up in these mumsy places, it gives less confident men a boost to attend. And gradually they do...

4. If the good things that are on offer

through midwives or Children's Centres clash with your working hours and you can't get flexibility to attend, ask whether they can offer stuff in the evening or at weekends.

5. Do you have skills the place could use? For example, if you are a chef, you could run a cooking session. If you are a builder you could help out.

6. Volunteer to help with the children. You will need to get a CRB (Criminal Records Bureau) check to do this, of course. You probably won't ever again have the opportunity to be surrounded by such tiny children. It's a real privilege.

7. Work your way in, don't be demanding. Complaining is a last resort! If staff are not friendly to you, be really friendly back. Look at www.fatherhoodinstitute.org.

8. If the whole place is *really* mumsy (such as a 'Mums and Tots' group that is definitely mums and tots!) and you are in a minority of one, consider being a trail-blazer father. Just go for it and be the one that is different.

Kitchen table talk
Questions to ask each other:

 **What do we do differently when it comes to parenting and is that OK?**

 What do you think I am best at with parenting?

 What do you think I could do better? (Does it feel safe for me even to ask this question?)

→ **Do I ever use stereotypes about what men and women should do to defend what I do, without discussing it with you?**

Chapter 5

Getting on with each other

relationship

money listening

depression sharing

talking sos

couple time sex

separation

The relationship between parents is important for children

Experts have shown that the relationship between parents has a really big influence on the future of the child. Yes, how good we are at parenting is important, and that's what we spend most of our time thinking about – 'am I a good mother?' 'am I a good father?' But if we sacrifice our relationship with each other for our children, it actually does not help them.

In a survey by the Children's Society, 70% of teenagers said that their parents getting on with each other was of great importance to their happiness, but only 30 per cent of parents thought this. The teenagers were right. It's very sad that we parents can so easily forget what once, as children, we knew.

In my work I often present the 'family triangle'.

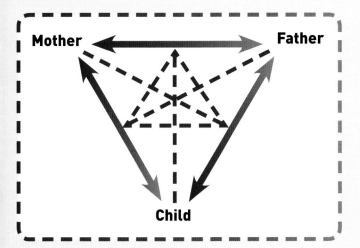

This shows how every member of the family and every relationship in a family is important; everything affects everything. It is *not* enough simply to be good at parenting.

Even if talking does not lead to big changes, we can sometimes feel better just because we have spoken out and been heard

Elizabeth Martyn, a Relate counsellor and author of *Babyshock! Your Relationship Survival Guide* has seen many couples in trouble. She writes: 'Once you have a baby you get on to this treadmill of babies/children and by the time you wake up 5 or 10 or 15 years later the problems are huge and you've just been sitting on them. People are so responsible about their parenting, but completely discount themselves and their relationship. They feel they can't say: "Go away children, we're going to do such and such." All these years they've just assumed their relationship will be OK, and then it falls apart.'

Many of the advice books on nurturing your relationship after you've had a baby say roughly the same things. It is all about:

- Talking and listening
- Sharing tasks
- Couple time
- Maintaining a good sex life
- Being fair with money
- Getting help early when things are getting out of hand

> **In a survey by the Children's Society, 70% of teenagers said that their parents getting on with each other was of great importance to their happiness, but only 30 per cent of parents thought this. The teenagers were right**

Let's start by doing the things that we hate least. What does that leave?
Are nappies really that expensive?!
Something's wrong. What is it?
We keep arguing. Can't we see if someone can help us to stop?
You look really miserable and I'm too tired. Shall we check it with the GP?

TALKING AND LISTENING

It works – as long as we talk when we're not fighting and angry and both of us are prepared to take turns to listen to each other. Even if talking does not lead to big changes at home, we can sometimes feel better with each other just because we've spoken out and been heard. When it comes to worries about our relationship, 'better out than in', as Shrek would say!

SHARING TASKS

The number one cause of arguments is about who does what in the house.

So how do we start the negotiations? These are things other parents have tried:

- The 'we-each-do-what-we-hate-the-least' principle
- The 'we-each-do-the-things-we-know-our partner-really-wants-done' principle
- The 'we-each-do-the-things-we-can't-stand-not-being-done' principle
- The 'jack-of-all-trades' method – we make sure we are both able to do everything (not for the faint hearted, this one)
- The 'absolute 50/50' method – for instance, we split the laundry, and alternate between the whites and coloureds on a weekly basis (best if this method is approached as a sport!)

- And never forget to consider the 'what-can-we-afford-to-pay-(or persuade)-other-people-to-do-for-us?' option.

None of these is guaranteed to work. The only thing researchers do know is that if parents regularly talk about who does what, agree stuff realistically, stick to their agreement (or re-negotiate) and appreciate each other's efforts, it's usually possible to muddle through without housework becoming a blow-out issue.

'US' TIME

- It is *not* selfish. It is necessary for our children.
- Make a regular time every week to talk and relax (not when you should be sleeping!)
- Make a regular time (perhaps once a month) to do something you enjoyed doing together before the children were born.

SEX – MAKE LOVE NOT WAR

Sex can go out of the window for a number of reasons when there are babies or small children:

- It can hurt after the birth
- She feels vulnerable and emotional after the birth
- It was uncomfortable during pregnancy
- We are too tired and stressed
- We are out of the habit
- The baby has not settled; a crying baby makes sex

pretty much impossible

- Mum and baby are inseparable; dad feels marginalised
- Lack of desire or feeling unattractive
- Depression
- Feeling different about our partner as a 'mother' or 'father'
- Or sometimes even: the baby is a good excuse for not carrying on a sex life that wasn't great anyway

Most couples get by on something in between total deprivation and what they had before!

If sex has not restarted after six months, sexual interest may have died down and it is a matter of reviving it. That may need expert help to restore – books or sex therapy. Talking about sex can be tricky, but there's lots of good stuff out there and talking is vital: not doing so is guaranteed to make the problem worse.

Also the following are worth trying:

- Hugs, cuddles and sensual massage with no sex can be really important for a while
- Getting back to sleeping in the same bed as soon as possible (if that stopped because of the baby)
- Going to bed earlier and at the same time as each other once in a while (easier said than done!)
- Having sex at an unusual time of the day (at a time when the baby is really settled and asleep) and not last thing at night when exhausted

- Getting grandparents or a friend to babysit at *their* house for an afternoon or evening
- Scheduling sex in and sticking to it. One couple regularly had what they called the 'duty bonk' and found that once they got started they tended to enjoy it
- Finding a counsellor or a manual
- Seeing a GP if sex continues to be painful
- *Not* doing it if it really makes one parent distressed – but, in that case, seek help!

Help

- Relate, 0300 100 1234, www.relate.org.uk (Relate has access to lots of sex counsellors)

MONEY, MONEY, MONEY

Money is a really big one when it comes to arguments. Common issues are:

- Partners haven't agreed spending priorities
- One partner has no idea how much some things really cost – whether servicing the car or buying baby food
- The lower earner loses independence and control of the spending
- One partner thinks the other spends selfishly on themselves

- One partner thinks the other spends stupidly on the baby
- Changes in the power balance – especially if the mother returns to work
- The costs of childcare

What's particularly interesting, is that when there's simply not enough money coming in, the couple may not focus on this real problem: instead, they can start to blame each other for everything else.

Help

- www.direct.gov.uk (has masses of financial advice)
- The local Citizens Advice Bureau, www.adviceguide.org.uk
- National Debtline, 0800 808 4000, www.nationaldebtline.co.uk

DEPRESSION

A word about depression, because it has a massive impact on our relationships if it happens.

We all hear about postnatal depression in mothers, but the fact is that for every two mothers who get it, one father gets it. *And* depression can happen before the baby is born too. What's more, if one of the parents gets it, the other is more likely to get it, because having a depressed partner is, well, depressing... Having a baby piles on enough pressures as it is, without our partner becoming unable to cope.

BE AWARE: many health professionals won't ask how a father is doing. If he is depressed it may take a lot longer for anyone to notice – he will not be coping well and the baby's mother will feel even more responsible (and probably angry, too). A depressed father may try to hide it (from himself, as well as from his partner) by staying out of the home.

And if it's the mother who is depressed, the father may not be offered the help he needs to support her.

There's a great case study of depression in a father on the website of the Fatherhood Institute, www.fatherhoodinstitute.org/index.php?id=2&cID=264

Depression is more than the 'baby blues', which mothers in particular commonly experience in the first day or two after the birth and which usually pass quite quickly.

Symptoms of depression can include:

- Feeling wretched and despairing
- Being irritable and angry
- Being very tired – so exhausted that it is like being physically ill
- Not sleeping well
- Not being hungry
- Not interested in anything
- Not interested in sex
- Unable to organise things and make routines
- Feeling guilty at being a failure

- Feeling anxious about anything and everything
- Burying ourselves in work (or in drink, drugs, computer games or some other obsessive hobby)

Depression is much better handled if both parents are alert to it and can work out ways of supporting the other through it:

- Finding people to talk to if either parent is depressed: friends, family, midwife, health visitor, GP
- Helping the depressed partner with quiet time to connect with the baby
- Couple time, when the baby is safely with another carer
- Really, really trying not to blame each other
- Getting the depressed person assessed by a GP
- Putting off any other big life changes if possible, such as moving house

Help (for mums)

- Royal Society of Psychiatrists, www.rcpsych.ac.uk
- Association for Post-Natal Illness, www.apni.org

Help (for dads)

- Dad Info, www.dad.info.

Help (for both)

- Your GP

SOS – GETTING RELATIONSHIP HELP WHEN WE NEED IT

All relationships could use a little help sometimes. When we need help, we may need to be brave, admit it and do something about it.

There are lots of great books and websites that can help get the most out of parenting and our relationship:

- *Partnership Parenting* (by Kyle Pruett and Marsha Kline Pruett, American publisher)
- *Babyshock! Your Relationship Survival Guide* (by Elizabeth Martyn, published by Relate)
- www.thecoupleconnection.net – a private on-line space with self-help tools (all very confidential!)
- www.relateforparents.org.uk – info and access to confidential advice
- www.letssticktogether.co.uk – tips on how not to fall out completely; some funny videos on what not to do in an argument

DIVORCE AND SEPARATION

Cooperating around parenting does not always mean staying together. But if couples do decide to divorce or separate, it *does* mean that we have to keep the fighting to a minimum and never slag our partner off, not only in front of the child, but in our own mind. And the smallest babies are sensitive to rows in the house.

Some useful books and websites to help parents who are not happy are:

- *The Guide for Separated Parents: putting your children first* (by Karen and Nick Woodall)
- *Moving on: Breaking Up without Breaking Down* (by Suzie Hayman, published by Relate)
- *For the Sake of the Children* (by Sue Secker)
- The Couple Connection, www.thecoupleconnection.net
- Relate, www.relateforparents.org.uk, 0300 100 1234
- Family Wizard, www.ourfamilywizard.com
- Child Maintenance Options, www.cmoptions.org, a website which addresses 'common separation concerns'
- Resolution, www.resolution.org.uk/ parentingafterparting

Kitchen table talk
Some of the tricky questions:

 **Is one of us always on the other's back when they are looking after the children? Is one of us withdrawing from things that need doing?**

 Does either of us regularly criticize the other – not just about childcare, but lots of things, including their personality?

 Is one of us staying at work too much? Are we spending enough time together?

 Post-baby, how do we want our sex life to be?

Chapter 6

Is sharing care of children natural? What did we do when we lived in caves?

ancestors

hormones

chimpanzees

marmoset monkeys

extended families

flexibility

working mothers

Sharing is natural

When parents take very traditional roles within their families, they sometimes say that these roles are hard-wired. It is natural – the way we did it when we lived in caves, is their reasoning. As one father put it in the *Daily Mail* recently, 'We chaps feel the same way about childcare as our grunting, hairy, mammoth-hunting ancestors did.'

But is this straight division of labour that the man works and the woman cares how our ancestors really lived in the caves, woodlands and on the plains that they used to call home? I decided to find out what cavemen and cavewomen actually did. Were there terraces of dwellings, each a home to mum, dad and cavebaby?

What I found surprised me a lot.

A brilliant and fascinating book, called
Mothers and Others by Sarah Blaffer
Hrdy, (a Professor of Anthropology at
University of California, Davis), looks
at how children have been brought up
since we evolved into human beings
– and sharing turns out to be normal,
natural and necessary.

How mothers have cared for children

Hrdy explains that for the last 200,000 years mothers have worked – very hard. It all started when we lived in the earliest of crude shelters in Africa. Hunting for meat could never bring in enough calories to survive on – foraging was always essential; in short, everyone helped get the food. In all communities except a few wealthy ones, everyone has worked – all the time.

In human families, mothers have shared the care with others within their families and sometimes with others outside the family – for most of our existence we have lived in large extended families, with lots of women and men to share the work of caring for children. Human children take a very long time to raise compared to other animals. They are very hard work and raising them takes a big family effort – and largely because we, as a species, have been so good at this kind of sharing and cooperation, we have thrived.

Species vary a lot in how they bring up babies, even among apes and monkeys who are closest to us. Chimpanzee babies stick totally to their mothers and die pretty quickly if they don't, but other primates do things very differently. Colobus monkey mothers share the care with other females. Titi monkey mothers hand the babies to the father when not feeding the baby milk, and run off to look for food. Marmoset and Tamarin male monkeys put on weight during the mother's pregnancy so they can do without food when the (twin) babies are born – they'll spend most of their time holding the babies so the mother can eat and keep her milk-supply up.

For most of our existence we have lived in large extended families, with lots of women and men to share the work of caring for children

How babies thrive on many carers

As long as they have a strong close relationship with at least one carer, human babies and childen thrive on being cared for by several people. Babies are very good at making adults fall in love with them. They are very sensitive to how adults in the family get on with each other. Babies and children know where they will get the most love and the best care. Hrdy believes that it is actually very good for babies to have to encourage (with smiles, cries and other baby-skills) more than one carer to help look after them. This helps babies become more sociable.

Grandad's upstairs gazing at baby - he's hooked!
I'm just going to kill a mammoth. Can you dig some veg?
Just how many aunts and uncles does it take to give baby a bath?!
Can we stop talking and watch a DVD?
I'll stay in camp with the babies and do some exercise till I can throw my spear again.
Can we talk?

How fathers have joined in (sometimes)

In human beings, far more than in any other species, the involvement of fathers has been and is incredibly variable. Sometimes human fathers are totally involved – for instance, the hunter gatherer Aka tribe in Central Africa, where fathers spend nearly a quarter of their whole time holding their babies!

In other societies, men are not directly involved with infants at all, or their involvement is very little. They may work long distances away and send money home. They go off to die in wars. They work close to home but things are organized so that they have little involvement – particularly with very young children.

Sometimes human fathers are totally involved and sometimes their involvement is very little

It seems that human families specialize in flexibility – they can operate in very different ways in response to very different conditions. When men are needed as carers, they can be switched into caring. Like women, they are programmed to react to babies. The hormones linked to love, tolerance, trust and sensitivity to babies – oxytocin and prolactin – increase in fathers within minutes of holding their baby. Living in the same house as a pregnant woman can also cause these hormones to kick in. The more men are at home and the more they handle their babies, the more their hormones tend to change when faced with a baby – nature seems to be tying them to their job of caring.

The hormones linked to love increase within minutes of a man holding his baby

Human parenting since 200,000 BC

As already pointed out, since the beginning of the human race, mothers have shared the load of caring for children. The guilt that many of today's mothers feel about not being there 100 per cent probably comes largely from the 1950s when governments were keen for women to have lots of babies to replace the generation wiped out in the Second World War and the paying jobs were needed for men returning from war.

So, a mother staying at home in a small family unit by herself to look after children is very unusual compared to the way we've been operating over the last 200,000 years. If the time-line for the whole human race were 24 hours, the 'mum at home/dad at work' model started about 30 seconds ago. This model can work for some families if the mother has lots of local support but the fact is, it's really unusual.

Now we are at another moment in history when fathers are needed for the caring of children. Most children in this country are not brought up in large extended families with lots of adults around to care for children. They are born in small family units where the father is the closest person on hand to join in the caring. Meanwhile, women are just as good at earning money as men these days, and the family usually needs them to work.

If the time-line for the whole human race were 24 hours, the 'mum at home/dad at work' model started about 30 seconds ago

But nearly every month, some piece of research is reported in the media and is said to prove to mothers that working outside the home is damaging their children's health or ruining their children's life chances. But if we asked the right question – 'do children do OK when they are well looked after by mother, father and other carers working together?' we get a very different answer. And the answer is – yes, they do! The children who do badly are those who don't get very good care, whether it's from their mother, their father, or from other carers – at home, at nursery, wherever. It's the quality of care from a range of people that matters, and how supportive the network of care is, not whether mum works or not.

It's the quality of care from a range of people that matters, not whether mum works or not

That's why some children with full-time mothers actually do worse than children looked after by fathers, grandparents, nannies, childminders or nursery staff. If their mother is depressed, lonely, unsupported, then she can't give the best care. And the same goes for fathers: if a father is trying to care for his children and he's feeling depressed, lonely and unsupported, then that won't be doing them good either.

So the lesson from human history is that raising children is not just mothers' business. It is family business. Fathers are well equipped to do this 'by nature' and are particularly needed right now for caring just as mothers are particularly needed for earning. That is why it is so important for children that we look at how parents work together – which is why I wrote this book.

> **If the mother feels depressed, lonely and unsupported, then she can't give the best care. The same goes for fathers**

Kitchen table talk

If anyone has got to this point in the book and discussed everything, it's time for a beer and some TV!

But of course, you are more than welcome to join the discussions on www.whodoeswhatbook.com to see what other people have thought of this book.